STUDIES IN SOCIOLOGY

This series, prepared under the auspice[s]
Association, is designed to provide sho[rt]
scholarly treatments of key problem-areas in sociology. The books
do not offer summary accounts of the current state of research in
various fields, but seek rather to analyse matters which are the
subject of controversy or debate. The series is designed to cover a
broad range of topics, falling into three categories: (1) abstract
problems of social theory and social philosophy; (2) interpretative
questions posed by the writings of leading social theorists; (3) issues
in empirical sociology. In addition, the series will carry translations
of important writings in sociology which have not previously been
available in English. Each book makes a substantive contribution
to its particular topic, while at the same time giving the reader an
indication of the main problems at issue; each carries an annotated
bibliography, comprising a critical survey of relevant further
literature.

ANTHONY GIDDENS

University of Cambridge

STUDIES IN SOCIOLOGY

General Editor: ANTHONY GIDDENS

Editorial Advisers: T. B. BOTTOMORE, DAVID LOCKWOOD and ERNEST GELLNER

Published

POLITICS AND SOCIOLOGY IN THE THOUGHT OF MAX WEBER
Anthony Giddens

PROFESSIONS AND POWER
Terence J. Johnson

THE SOCIAL PROCESS OF INNOVATION: A STUDY IN THE SOCIOLOGY
OF SCIENCE
M. J. Mulkay

Forthcoming

THE SOCIOLOGY OF SOCIAL MOVEMENTS
J. Banks

MARXIST SOCIOLOGY
T. B. Bottomore

MATHEMATICS AND SOCIOLOGY
B. Hindess

STRIKES AND INDUSTRIAL CONFLICT
G. Ingham

THE DEVELOPMENT OF THE SOCIOLOGY OF KNOWLEDGE
S. Lukes

CONSCIOUSNESS AND ACTION IN THE WESTERN WORKING CLASS
M. Mann

MICHELS AND THE CRITIQUE OF SOCIAL DEMOCRACY
F. Parkin

The Social Process of Innovation

A study in the sociology of science

M. J. MULKAY
Assistant Director of Research, Engineering Department
University of Cambridge

Macmillan

First published 1972 by
THE MACMILLAN PRESS LTD
London and Basingstoke
Associated companies in New York Toronto
Dublin Melbourne Johannesburg and Madras

SBN 333 13431 1

Printed in Great Britain by
THE ANCHOR PRESS LTD
Tiptree, Essex

CONTENTS

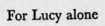

For Lucy alone

1. INTRODUCTION

From the seventeenth to the middle of the twentieth century the number of those engaged in scientific research increased at an ever-faster rate in most Western societies. As their numbers expanded, so these men and their special knowledge became more and more important for the achievement of practical goals, such as economic growth and success in war, and for the development of other intellectual spheres. In view of the rapid and cumulative growth of science and its great impact on thought and technology, it is surprising how little is known about the social processes whereby scientific information is generated, accepted as valid by the research community and, finally, passed on to the wider society. One important reason for the lack of systematic knowledge in this area is that reference to the way in which ideas develop is rigorously suppressed in scientific textbooks and even more so in the papers presented to professional journals.[1] Another factor is that researchers trained in non-scientific disciplines find it difficult to understand the intellectual complexities of modern science; while scientists themselves, although less harassed by this difficulty, are seldom willing to devote much effort to the detailed study of their own and their colleagues' professional activities. Nevertheless, in recent years a body of literature has begun to form concerned with depicting the social processes of scientific innovation. Some of it has come from persons trained as natural scientists (e.g. Kuhn, 1962); rather more has come from social scientists (e.g. Merton, 1957); while occasionally representatives of both groups have collaborated (e.g. Reif and Strauss, 1965). My aim in the following pages will be to build an interpretative framework, based upon this literature and my own studies, which will act as a fruitful guide for further sociological investigation of scientific innovation.

[1] The reasons for this are explored in Kuhn (1962, 1963).

For the sake of clarity, let me state briefly the way in which the argument presented below is organised. The section following this introduction contains a description of a series of innovations made by Pasteur. This material is presented at the beginning because the events described exemplify many of the social processes to be examined subsequently in detail. Thus assertions in later sections are often illustrated by brief reference to the discussion of Pasteur. An attempt is also made in this section to demonstrate that scientific communities frequently display a rigid orthodoxy and that deviation from the current orthodoxy is usually discouraged. In Section 3 it is argued that intellectual conformity is initially engendered by the system of professional training in science and effectively maintained within the research community by processes of social exchange. Section 4 contains the kernel of the analysis. Its central thesis is that the very processes of social exchange which, under certain conditions, work to maintain intellectual conformity, themselves regularly generate new conditions favouring innovation. Two main types of innovation are discussed: that involving 'revolutionary' replacement of firmly established orthodoxies, and that involving intellectual migration. The discussion is completed in Section 5 where it is suggested that, as a result of the processes of social exchange, significant innovation emerges mainly at the top and the bottom of the status hierarchy of science. Throughout the analysis I have concentrated on examining how new information is generated by social processes occurring within the research community and how members of this community come to accept or reject the information presented to them. I have paid little attention to social factors originating outside the research community and I have dealt solely with 'basic research', that is, with research activity the results of which are submitted for publication in the professional scientific journals. Furthemore, the discussion has been limited to scientific developments occurring in Western Europe and North America since approximately the middle of the last century. Lastly, although my main concern has been the physical and biological sciences, much of the analysis may well apply to other academic disciplines.

2. THE RECEPTION OF PASTEUR'S INNOVATIONS: COGNITIVE AND TECHNICAL NORMS

It might seem fitting to begin a study of the social process of scientific innovation by asking the question: how is new information generated within the research community? I wish to start less directly, however, by examining the way in which new information is accepted or rejected. Before discussing these latter processes in general terms, I shall describe a series of innovations made by Pasteur and the responses of the scientific community to these innovations. Towards the end of this section I shall use this material to show that there are intellectual orthodoxies in science and that new ideas are accepted more easily the more consistent they are with the existing orthodoxy.

In 1846 Pasteur began studying the ability of organic substances to rotate the plane of polarised light, and to investigate the connection between this property and the crystal structure and molecular configuration of organic substances. Research of this kind had been undertaken in France since the beginning of the century and similar problems were being pursued elsewhere when Pasteur started work. There was, in fact, a well-established tradition of research in the area. Certain techniques were widely accepted; for example, use of the microscope and of the goniometer for observing crystalline forms. Problems were clearly stated; for example, is there a relation between the crystalline structure of quartz and the way in which it rotates the plane of polarised light? Finally, the solutions obtained were usually unequivocal: for instance, quartz rotates light to the right and to the left because quartz crystals have both right- and left-handed facets.

It was in this intellectual climate that Pasteur tried to resolve an anomaly posed by Mitscherlich in 1844. At that time two different forms of tartaric acid were recognised, tartaric and paratartaric acid. Mitscherlich had found that these two acids and their salts, the tartrates and paratartrates, had the same chemical composition, the same crystal structure, and so on. So far as he had been able to observe, they were identical except that the tartrate solution rotated the plane of polarisation, while that of the paratartrate was optically inactive. Pasteur decided that, in the light of current scientific knowledge, the two substances could not really be chemically identical and he decided to work on the assumption that any chemical difference between tartrates and paratartrates would be revealed by differences in the shape of their crystals. More specifically, he assumed that whereas the crystal of the optically inert paratartrate would be symmetrical, that of the tartrate would have some irregularity linked to the rotation of polarised light. The latter part of this hypothesis was quickly confirmed by observation. However, when he turned to the paratartrates,

> he found facets similar to those present on the crystals of optically active tartrates. Still intent on finding a difference he noticed that while the facets were all turned towards the right in the tartrate, in the case of paratartrate crystals some were turned to the right, and some to the left. Obeying the promptings of his hypothesis, he sedulously picked out the right-handed crystals and placed them in one heap, and the left-handed crystals in another, dissolved each group in water, and then examined the two solutions separately in the polarimeter – with results which made of this simple operation one of the classical experiments of chemical science. The solution of the right-handed crystals turned the plane of polarisation to the right, the solution of the left-handed crystals to the left. When the two solutions were mixed in equal amounts, the mixture proved optically inert.[1]

Pasteur's results were quickly communicated to Biot, who had opened up this field of research some forty years earlier. The latter was so sceptical that he would not accept the findings until they had been demonstrated in his presence. When this had been done,

[1] R. J. Dubos, *Louis Pasteur: Free Lance of Science* (London: Gollancz, 1951) pp. 94–5.

10

however, and when he was sure that Pasteur had properly used the correct techniques, Biot was immediately convinced. He agreed enthusiastically to present and defend Pasteur's paper before the Académie des Sciences and became, for the rest of his life, Pasteur's scientific sponsor. With Biot's support, Pasteur's work was quickly absorbed by the scientific community.

Pasteur's first crystallographic research was accepted with little opposition for several reasons. In the first place, he tackled a problem which was generally regarded as legitimate and significant. Secondly, his research techniques were well established, although he used them in a novel way. Thirdly, his findings, although unexpected, were relatively unambiguous as well as consistent with widespread assumptions about the relation between crystalline form and optical rotation. As a result of factors like these, plus Biot's sponsorship, the response to Pasteur's work was favourable. Thus in the case where Pasteur combined innovation, in the sense of providing new and unexpected information, with overall conformity to current scientific conceptions, acceptance was almost immediate. This was less true, however, of much of his later research.

After some years spent pursuing the implications of his work on tartaric acid and molecular and crystalline dissymmetry, Pasteur began to generalise some of his findings. ' "The universe", he said one day, "is a dissymmetrical whole. I am inclined to think that life ... must be a function of the dissymmetry of the universe. . . ." '[1] Acting on this inference, Pasteur devised a series of experiments designed to bring dissymmetrical forces to bear upon chemical and biological phenomena. For instance, he used powerful magnets to attempt to introduce dissymmetry into the form of crystals. He constructed a clockwork mechanism to keep plants in continual rotation, first in one direction, then in another, and he tried to keep plants alive under the influence of solar rays reversed by means of a mirror directed by a heliostat. These projects alarmed his mentors and colleagues by their radical departure from current scientific preconceptions. The problems posed by Pasteur were decreed fantastic and the techniques unprecedented. Almost without exception his fellow scientists tried to dissuade him from continuing with this research, and after some months of largely fruitless effort Pasteur did move on to the problem of fermenta-

[1] Cited in R. Vallery-Radot, *Life of Pasteur* (London : Constable, 1906) p. 72.

tion. He did not, however, abandon the prejudice that molecular dissymmetry was associated with the forces of life. Consequently, he was sure in advance that the processes of fermentation, which gave evidence of molecular dissymmetry, were associated with the activity of living organisms.

When Pasteur came to study fermentation, the preconceptions which he brought with him differed considerably from the view currently accepted in the field. By 1850 most scientists regarded fermentations as caused by chemical agents alone. Although in popular thought fermentation had widely been associated with the processes of life, the chemists of the eighteenth and early nineteenth centuries tried to account for it solely in terms of the chemical reactions which were proving so successful in describing other natural phenomena. Some investigators argued against the purely chemical interpretation of fermentation on the grounds that fermentation only occurred in the presence of living organisms, for example yeast. In 1835 Cagniard de la Tour and Schwann independently published results which they regarded as showing that alcoholic fermentation was closely associated with the organic growth of yeast cells. But these ideas were so contrary to the prevailing, purely chemical view of fermentation that they were simply rejected without serious consideration :

These three papers were received with incredulity and Berzelius, at that time the arbiter of the chemical world, reviewed them all with impartial scorn in his *Jahresbericht* for 1839. . . .

To the scorn of Berzelius was soon added the sarcasm of Wöhler and Liebig. At the request of the Académie des Sciences, Turpin of Paris had repeated in 1839 Cagniard de la Tour's observations and confirmed their accuracy. Stimulated by this publication, Wöhler prepared an elaborate skit, which he sent to Liebig, who added to it some touches of his own and published it in the *Annalen der Chemie*, following immediately upon a translation of Turpin's paper. Yeast was here described, with a considerable degree of anatomical realism, as consisting of eggs which developed into minute animals shaped like distilling apparatus.[1]

These attempts by those in positions of eminence and authority

[1] Dubos, *Louis Pasteur*, p. 121.

to discredit intellectual nonconformity indicate clearly the existence of strong convictions among research chemists at this period,
convictions which denied the relevance of living organisms to fermentation. There is not space here to examine in detail Pasteur's
innovations in this field. Broadly speaking, however, the facts
are as follows. In 1855 Pasteur began research on fermentation
with a strong, though as yet unproved, preconception that living
organisms were involved. After certain preliminary researches he
proposed the thesis that each type of fermentation was brought
about by a distinct micro-organism. Pasteur himself acknowledged that his arguments were inconclusive. Nevertheless, he
defended them vigorously against the attacks of chemists such as
Liebig, Berzelius and Wöhler, who had condemned the earlier
vitalist accounts of fermentation and who continued to attack
Pasteur's claims. The ensuing controversy over the character of
fermentation was acrimonious, and many of Pasteur's opponents
never altered their views even though, after some years of research,
debate and controversy, Pasteur's interpretation of fermentation
came to be widely accepted. But this acceptance was not due
simply to Pasteur's experimental skill or to the validity of his
explanation. It was also brought about by the influence of
Pasteur's growing reputation, by the sponsorship of eminent
academicians, and by the vigour with which Pasteur undertook
his campaign of persuasion. The relevance of such social factors
to the acceptance of Pasteur's views on fermentation can be seen
clearly in the revival of the controversy which occurred years
later on the death of the eminent physiologist Claude Bernard.
Among the latter's notes were some statements criticising Pasteur
and endorsing views on fermentation similar to those of Liebig.
These notes furnished no new evidence. They were little more
than a programme for further research. Yet the prestige of the
dead scientist was itself enough to put in jeopardy Pasteur's care-
fully supported conclusions, at least in the eyes of those still sus-
picious of a vitalist theory of fermentation. 'Thus began a weird
controversy, in which one of the main protagonists was in the
grave and appeared only in the form of a few posthumous notes.'[1]
This controversy was, of course, short-lived. That it occurred at
all was due to several factors: firstly, to the lasting commitment
of many researchers to a purely chemical view of fermentation;

[1] Ibid., p. 198.

secondly, to the fact that Pasteur's claims were presented without conclusive evidence; and thirdly, to the fact that much of the dispute was a result of the use by both sides of an ambiguous terminology.

In 1859, after having resolved many of the problems of fermentation, Pasteur altered the focus of his research to test the claim put forward by Pouchet that new living organisms are sometimes 'called into life' without parents. In such cases, Pouchet argued, organisms are not the result of 'normal' processes of reproduction. They are rather spontaneously 'drawn from the surrounding matter'. The basic issue here was whether the micro-organisms responsible for phenomena like fermentation, putre-faction and moulds appeared spontaneously in the appropriate substances or whether they were introduced from the air. The issue was far from clear-cut, however, especially as most pro-ponents of spontaneous generation argued that oxygen from the air, though not microbes, was required for generation to occur. The whole area was widely regarded as obscure, and when Pasteur announced his decision to investigate the problem his colleagues once more tried to dissuade him. But Pasteur would not change his mind. He began a series of experiments designed to show conclusively that spontaneous generation did not take place. Pasteur tried to establish that when flasks of fermentable fluid were freed of micro-organisms and removed from contact with air, organisms did not reappear in the fluid. Pouchet and others of Pasteur's opponents, using similar techniques, tried to show that, although oxygen was necessary for generation to occur, life did regularly emerge out of inanimate matter.

The controversy had now reached beyond the scientific arena. . . . Writers and publicists took sides in the polemic, not on the basis of factual evidence, but only under the influence of emotional and prejudiced beliefs. Despite his indignation at the war being conducted against him in the scientific bodies as well as in the daily press, Pasteur managed to control his temper for a few months; he judged it wiser to wait for a tactical error of his adversaries that would expose them to his blows.[1]

Pasteur's opportunity came when Pouchet accepted his chal-

[1] Ibid., pp. 172–3.

lenge on a specific point. Pasteur argued that when a number of sterile flasks of fermentable fluid were opened at high altitudes where microbes were few, and then immediately sealed, organic contamination would be relatively low and many of the flasks would remain unaltered. Pouchet argued that as soon as there was contact between air and fermentable fluid, spontaneous generation would occur. Pasteur used yeast infusion as his putrescible material and showed that the mixtures became putrid less frequently at altitudes where microbes were scarce. Pouchet used hay infusion and found that all his flasks revealed the development of living germs even when opened at high altitudes. At Pasteur's request a commission was formed by the Académie des Sciences to pass judgement. After some prevarication, Pouchet and his colleagues refused to accept the commission's terms and withdrew from the contest. The Academy then issued an authoritative statement in favour of Pasteur which effectively suppressed opinions in support of spontaneous generation for some years, especially in France. A decade later, however, Bastian, an English physician, put forward the thesis once more in extreme form. As Bastian received support from both scientists and laymen, Pasteur and others were forced to undertake further research, in the course of which many new problems were revealed and several old problems reopened. For instance, it was found that Pouchet's observations on hay infusion had been correct, although these observations did not actually demonstrate the occurrence of spontaneous generation. The commission had in fact based its authoritative statement on insufficient evidence. It was some years before all the ambiguities associated with spontaneous generation were finally cleared up to the satisfaction of all microbiologists and an intellectual consensus achieved, strong enough to withstand contrary claims from persons outside the research community.

Several important points about the reception of scientific information emerge from this description of some of Pasteur's discoveries. Firstly, research is in many cases guided by cognitive and technical assumptions which are generally endorsed by those working in the particular field. These assumptions operate as cognitive and technical norms (Mulkay, 1969). They define which problems and techniques are legitimate and what kinds of solutions are acceptable. The existence of cognitive and technical norms is clear in the case of the coherent tradition of research on problems of crystalline form and optical rotation as well as that of chemical research on fermentation. Thus those working in either of these areas, although often widely separated geographically and without direct intellectual contact, used similar techniques, chose related and often identical problems, and quickly reached similar assessments of research findings. Secondly, radical departure from current cognitive and/or technical norms, like other forms of social deviance, usually provokes attempts at social control. This is evident in the informal pressures put upon Pasteur to abandon research on molecular dissymmetry and on spontaneous generation. It is also clear in the attempts by Liebig and Wöhler to discredit the vitalist interpretation of fermentation. Thirdly, social factors such as sponsorship and prestige can influence the reception of deviant ideas in science. Several examples are given above: the conservative effect of statements about fermentation by Liebig and Berzelius; the way in which Biot, Dumas and others helped to ease the passage of Pasteur's innovations; the way in which Pasteur himself defeated Pouchet; and the impact of Bernard's notes on scientific opinion about fermentation. Fourthly, the degree of ambiguity of cognitive norms and the extent to which they are endorsed by those working in the field vary over time and from one research specialty to another. These latter factors also seem to affect the way in which innovations are received. Thus within the research network concerned with molecular structure and optical rotation, cognitive expectations were well defined, anomalous findings clearly perceived, and legitimate solutions quickly absorbed throughout the network. In contrast, work on spontaneous generation was undertaken from a great variety of intellectual perspectives by people both within and outside the research community. In this situation of intellectual and social openness it was for many years impossible to achieve either a clear definition of problems or general use of reliable techniques. Because cognitive and technical norms were so vague and because effective intellectual control could not be maintained over such a diffuse body of contributors, the debate over spontaneous generation was lengthy, acrimonious and confused – quite unlike the steady accumulation of knowledge about crystalline form and optical rotation.

The broad conclusion to be drawn from the discussion so far is that new information will be accepted more easily the more it accords with current cognitive and technical norms, the more widespread is agreement about these norms by those engaged in

16

research, and the more precise these norms are. This conclusion is significant because there is a strong tendency for cognitive norms to become increasingly precise within any given area of scientific research, and for those who are not strongly committed to these norms to be prevented from contributing information. Thus Conant (1951) has shown that many scientific disciplines and specialties, after starting with rather vague and commonsense notions, increasingly achieve a precise intellectual consensus. Ziman (1968) similarly has proposed that scientific communities are distinguished from other intellectual communities, primarily by the degree of their intellectual consensus and by the cognitive precision which they achieve through narrow specialisation. Kuhn (1962) also has argued very forcefully that scientific research is guided by relatively precise cognitive schemes or paradigms, that in most instances there is almost universal acceptance of the current paradigm, and that this consensus is achieved at least partly by exclusion of nonconformists.

The intellectual and social closure of research communities is largely responsible for the rapid accumulation of scientific knowledge. This is so for several reasons. Firstly, the need for constant concern with basic, and therefore indeterminate, issues is eliminated, at least for long periods. Secondly, while consensus is maintained, effort is no longer wasted in controversy between opposing schools. Thirdly, participants are united in a search for common intellectual goals and are able to investigate a narrow range of phenomena in great detail by means of specially designed equipment. Fourthly, information furnished by independent members of the network contributes to the intellectual needs of the group as a whole. These consequences of scientific consensus promote the rapid growth of bodies of precise knowledge. At the same time, however, such consensus tends, as we have seen, to suppress fundamental novelties. If we are to understand how significant innovation occurs none the less, we must first examine in some detail the mechanisms whereby intellectual conformity is maintained in science.

17

3. SOCIAL CONTROL IN SCIENCE

'At the root of the sociological theory of the development of science is the strategic fact of the multiple and independent appearance of the same scientific discovery' (Merton, 1961, p. 475). In the paper from which this quotation is taken, Merton distinguishes discoveries which are made once (singletons) from those which are made several times by independent researchers (multiples). He goes on to argue that multiples occur more often than singletons in science, although this fact is obscured by the practice of recognising only that claimant who first submits his information to the research community. Merton does not succeed in showing conclusively that multiples *predominate* in science He does demonstrate, however, that they occur frequently and that their occurrence is a distinctive feature of scientific development. This evidence adds support to the argument put forward in the previous section. For if the members of any given research community conform to certain cognitive and technical norms, we would expect them to choose closely related problems, use the same research techniques and, consequently, produce similar results. This line of argument may seem to conflict with the very evident demand for originality which exists within science (Merton, 1957). But originality is not valued unconditionally in science, as we have seen in the case of Pasteur. It is valued only in so far as it contributes to the predictable extension of the existing body of knowledge. Furthermore, whereas major innovations tend to be resisted strenuously, in many fields findings are regarded as original as long as they are not exactly duplicated in the existing literature.[1] There is, therefore, a bias against radical changes of perspective and in favour of the gradual accumulation

[1] M. J. Mulkay and A. T. Williams, 'A Sociological Study of a Physics Department', *British Journal of Sociology*, xxii 1 (Mar 1971) 68–82.

of detailed information within the limits of the current research framework. Thus the frequency of multiples, the recurrent resistance to innovations and the often minimal definition of 'originality' indicate the existence of strong pressures towards intellectual conformity in science. This conformity is maintained in three ways: through socialisation, through the exercise of authority, and by means of social exchange. I shall examine in turn these three aspects of social control in science.

All potential members of the scientific community are required to spend several years learning the body of established knowledge. During this period of formal education students are regularly assessed and those unable to comprehend or unwilling to accept as valid the existing corpus of knowledge are rigorously excluded. This, of course, is true of all academic fields. The sciences do appear to differ, however, in the rigidity with which they present their material and the strict intellectual conformity which in general they demand of their students. There is a growing body of evidence to support this statement. For example, a recent British study of chemistry undergraduates describes how these students are required to absorb uncritically an immense array of facts.[1] Similarly Jevons (1969, p. 140), bringing together a wide range of evidence, concludes that often 'studying science becomes stenography plus memorisation'. When students are not being taught established facts and associated theories they are learning how to get the correct answers to precise problems set in terms of the current framework. Facts, theories and problems are typically contained in textbooks which present each body of material from a single, unquestioned perspective. The 'various textbooks that the student does encounter display different subject matters, rather than, as in many of the social sciences, exemplifying different approaches to a single problem field. Even books that compete for adoption in a single course differ mainly in level and in pedagogic detail, not in substance or conceptual structure' (Kuhn, 1963, p. 344). Moreover, science is seldom taught historically. Students acquire a solid knowledge of the end-product of research but little awareness of the uncertainties, ambiguities and varied intellectual possibilities of research itself. As Kuhn infers, no approach to education could be better calculated to produce rigid mental sets.

Further tentative support for this view is supplied by Hudson's

[1] *Nature,* ccxxviii (26 Dec 1970) 1242–4.

work (1966, 1968) on convergers and divergers. Hudson applied a series of mental tests to boys in the fourth, fifth and sixth forms of a number of English public and grammar schools. From the results of these tests he was able to classify about 30 per cent of the boys as convergers, i.e. they scored highly on tests where each question had one correct answer but rather poorly when questions could be answered from a variety of different perspectives. In contrast, the 30 per cent of so-called 'divergers' did relatively badly on rigidly structured tests but rather well on tests which required them to think 'fluently and tangentially'. This finding is relevant to the present discussion because Hudson also found that divergers tended to be arts students and convergers to be science students. There were, of course, many science students who were divergers. Moreover, students' classifications varied somewhat from one test to another. Nevertheless, the connection between science and convergence in this study was strong. Hudson summarises his findings as follows:

> Between three and four divergers go into arts subjects like history, English literature and modern languages for every one that goes into physical science. And vice versa, between three and four convergers do mathematics, physics and chemistry for every one that goes into the arts. (1966, pp. 56–7)

Hudson also presents preliminary evidence that convergent thinking becomes more pronounced during secondary education, that science students are more committed to the intellectual framework furnished by the school syllabus, and he refers to an American study in which it was found that science undergraduates also became increasingly convergent in the course of their university career. These findings are clearly consistent with the argument proposed above that the style of teaching in science promotes intellectual conformity.

One important point, however, must be stressed. It is not implied that science students are uncreative, that they are relatively incapable of producing new ideas or perceiving unexpected relationships. What is implied is that their creativity will tend to occur within a rigid framework of ideas which they have come to take for granted. Some of Hudson's later work makes this clear. For instance, when he modified his open-ended tests by asking for a specific number of responses and by giving examples, convergers became much more divergent. It appears, therefore, that convergent boys can diverge, but only when they are told to do so and are shown what kinds of responses are legitimate. This finding is particularly interesting if we relate it to the practice of graduate study in the sciences. Graduate study is necessary in part because it enables students to acquire up-to-date knowledge which has not yet reached the textbooks and to develop those experimental or mathematical tools required in advanced study. But it is also the period during which potential researchers learn which aspects of the existing intellectual framework may legitimately be regarded as problematic. Thus Krebs, a Nobel laureate, maintains that the greatest advantage to the graduate student of studying with an eminent scientist is that the latter is able to impart the ability to choose problems which are both legitimate and significant:

> . . . attitudes rather than knowledge are conveyed by the distinguished teacher. . . . How to select worthwhile soluble problems and how to create the tools required to achieve a solution is something that scientists learn from the great figures in science rather than from books.[1]

In general, then, it seems that a rigid formal education for science students at school and university is followed by a period of close association with a researcher of demonstrated competence, during which the student learns how to select and solve legitimate problems in an acceptable manner; in other words, he is taught how to make an original contribution to knowledge within the limits of cognitive and technical norms current in the relevant research network.

In its dealings with potential members the research community is rigidly authoritarian. Within the community, in contrast, there is strong commitment to norms prescribing intellectual autonomy. In particular, scientists expect to be allowed to choose their own research problems (Hagstrom, 1965, p. 105). This clearly limits the effectiveness of any attempt by those occupying positions of authority in science to impose intellectual agreement. Nevertheless, intellectual consensus has been achieved on occasion by the fiat of scientific authority. For instance, the controversy between

[1] H. A. Krebs, 'The Making of a Scientist', *Nature,* ccxv (30 Sep 1967) 1443.

Pouchet and Pasteur mentioned above was resolved by official action on the part of the French Académie des Sciences whose decision, although based on insufficient evidence, determined the course of research for a decade. There has been no systematic investigation into authority relations as a source of intellectual control within the research community. However, it seems likely that in the blatant form exemplified by the decision over spontaneous generation, the exercise of scientific authority is rare. Nevertheless, recent changes in the organisation of research within certain specialties have brought about a definite increase in social relationships involving formal authority.

In some fields, such as high-energy physics, the pressures for collaboration among researchers have become so great that all research is now undertaken by fairly large groups. For instance, Swatez (1970) describes a group made up of 23 Ph.D. physicists, 20 graduate and research assistants, plus about 170 technical and administrative personnel. Within this group there is an elaborate division of research tasks coupled with centralised co-ordination and planning of research. Although an attempt is made to maintain some freedom of problem selection, each individual's choice is considerably restricted by the requirements of the group as a whole. Within laboratories of this kind the scientist's traditional autonomy is limited by the need for close collaboration with colleagues and by the need to conform to the general policies of a large and costly research organisation. However, such research is largely confined to a small number of distinctive specialties. Apart from these specialties it appears that most university scientists, although increasingly involved in informal collaboration, are not engaged in bureaucratised research (Hagstrom, 1964). Furthermore, even in fields where group research predominates, each group is still subject to external intellectual constraints. Because there are always several groups working in a given area, any single group, if its contributions are to be generally accepted, must satisfy the cognitive and technical expectations of other groups over which its members have no direct control. Although intellectual consensus within one group may be due wholly or in part to the control employed by those in positions of authority, an intellectual consensus common to several competing groups must have some other source. In fact, such consensus is maintained mainly by those processes of social exchange which I shall now describe.

There is a growing body of evidence that within the scientific community information is exchanged for professional recognition. To put this more specifically, the evidence establishes four things: firstly, that scientists supply information to their colleagues; secondly, that they receive recognition in return; thirdly, that recognition is experienced as a reward; and fourthly, that recognition is forthcoming primarily for contributions which conform to current cognitive and technical norms. The first of these points is perhaps the easiest to establish, for there can be little doubt that the main requirement of the scientist's research role is the provision of information to those working in the same field. Information is supplied to and gleaned from the research community in several ways. For instance, scientists send each other private papers describing ongoing research as well as pre-prints of articles soon to be published. In addition, they attend conferences with the main objective of talking about their own work and of finding out what others in their area are doing. And in the United States particularly, the more eminent men regularly visit the major universities in order to keep abreast of current research. These informal channels of communication are supplemented by formal publication of findings in the professional journals. In fact, most of the information traded informally finds its way sooner or later into journal articles. But journals are not simply a means of communicating information. They are also centrally involved in establishing the value of research contributions and in distributing professional recognition. Evidence consistent with this assertion is supplied by a recent study of high-energy physicists in Britain (Gaston, 1969). In this study it was found, unexpectedly, that researchers seldom read the journals although they all strove to publish in them. This failure to use the journals as a source of information was due to the efficiency of the informal communication network. High-energy physicists did not read the journals because they had prior access to most of the published material. Nevertheless, although the informal network passed on information very efficiently, researchers continued to publish in the journals. It appears that they published, not solely to communicate their findings, but also to establish that their information was scientifically valuable (Hagstrom, 1965). The important difference between informal and formal communication is that the specialty exercises no control over the former, whereas in the latter case the journal, acting

23

on behalf of the research community, selects only that information which meets certain standards of competence and significance (Crane, 1967). Thus scientists seek to publish partly to establish that their work has met these standards and that it can therefore be regarded as a genuine contribution to certified knowledge.

There are several kinds of evidence, in addition to this study of high-energy physicists, which show that scientists publish in part to elicit a response from their colleagues and that this response takes the form of recognition of the scientific value of their contributions. In the first place, there is the fact that many researchers begin to feel anxious when they believe that somebody else is likely to anticipate their results. If scientists wished to extend the boundaries of knowledge for its own sake, this anxiety would not arise. It would not matter who got there first as long as the information was made available to the research community. Personal anxiety can arise only to the extent that each researcher wishes to establish that he, and no other, actually contributed the information. 'Scientists are concerned about being anticipated because they hope the solutions to their problems will interest other scientists, and, given this hope, it is only reasonable to expect other scientists to approach the same problems. . . . The concern over being anticipated arises because the scientist is . . . oriented toward achieving recognition and is afraid of not receiving it for work he has actually done' (Hagstrom, 1965, p. 72). A similar source of evidence that scientists publish in order to receive the reward of professional recognition is the occurrence of priority disputes in science. Priority disputes are arguments to determine, in situations where there is some doubt, who should be credited with first making a particular discovery. The award of priority to one scientist does not diminish the intellectual merit of those contenders who independently, but subsequently, arrived at the same result; nor does it reduce the satisfaction they derived from actually tackling and solving a difficult problem or from making an important discovery. None the less, bitter and prolonged disputes over priority have been peculiarly characteristic of the scientific community:

> . . . these controversies, far from being a rare exception in science, have long been frequent, harsh and ugly. They have practically become an integral part of the social relations between scientists. . . .

24

. . . When recognition of priority is either not granted or fades from view, the scientist loses his scientific property. Although this kind of property shares with other types general recognition of the 'owner's' rights, it contrasts sharply in all other respects. Once he has made his contribution, the scientist no longer has exclusive rights of access to it. It becomes part of the public domain of science. Nor has he the right of regulating its use by others by withholding it unless it is acknowledged as his. In short, property rights in science become whittled down to just this one : the recognition by others of the scientist's distinctive part in having brought the result into being. (Merton, 1957, pp. 449, 455–6)

A third source of relevant evidence is a paper by Reif (1961). Reif describes how the rapid growth of physics during the 1950s made it difficult for many researchers to gain proper credit for their work. 'When a "hot" subject breaks there is a deluge of follow-up contributions. . . . With the rapid exploitation of new ideas, priority questions become serious problems' (1961, p. 1957). The pressure on researchers to publish quickly and to establish priority became so great that many of them decided to secure their property rights by reporting their findings in short letters to the *Physical Review*. In due course this bi-monthly journal became so inundated with these notes, in addition to its full-length research reports, that a new journal was formed, the *Physical Review Letters*, 'devoted entirely to the fastest possible publication of short notes on important discoveries'. This response, however, did not resolve all the problems resulting from the competition to publish. For instance, within a year or two the editor of *Physical Review Letters* was forced to complain to his readers not only that he was receiving too many submissions whose meagre content did not justify publication even in the form of research notes, but also that some researchers were seeking to establish priority by announcing their results in the daily press. Reif comments that the scientist depends on the reputation he has established among other scientists for practically everything he does or hopes to attain, and that one effective way of attracting the attention of one's colleagues is by publishing as many papers as possible. Thus the pressure for accelerating the rate of publication, like priority disputes and anxiety over anticipation, is a byproduct of the exchange of information for recognition.

Let me summarise the findings described in the last few pages. Firstly, scientists continue to publish their work even when this is not strictly necessary for the purpose of communication. Secondly, they often vigorously defend their right to be given credit for significant contributions to knowledge. Thirdly, many of them are made anxious by the threat that routine research might be anticipated and their efforts go unrecognised. Fourthly, researchers sometimes strive to reduce this anxiety by speeding up the publication of their findings. These facts make sense only if we infer that researchers furnish information to their colleagues in order to elicit some valued response. Furthermore, the evidence strongly suggests that this valued response is the recognition, by those competent to judge, that the researcher has made a genuine contribution to science. Several additional considerations strengthen this interpretation. In the first place, scientists get nothing for publication other than recognition. Professional journals do not normally pay for contributions. In fact some of them actually charge contributors to help cover the costs of publication; while those which do pay tend to cater for a non-specialist audience and to be less favoured by the research community. Thus most research papers are offered as gifts to other interested researchers via the journals. It is sometimes argued that the scientist's main reward is neither money nor recognition but rather the pleasure derived from completing a successful piece of research. However, this argument is inconsistent with the regular occurrence of priority disputes and the prevalence of anxiety over anticipation. Furthermore, in the long run the only conclusive indication that a particular piece of work *is* valuable is the recognition granted by competent scientists. To meet the needs of its members for appropriate levels of recognition, the scientific community has evolved an elaborate hierarchy of awards (Merton, 1957). The most important of these forms of professional recognition are as follows: eponymy, that is, the practice of attaching a scientist's name to a particular scientific achievement – for example, the Mossbauer Effect, Darwinian Evolution, Planck's Constant; receipt of one of the enormous variety of prizes, three of the more well-known being the Nobel Prize, the Fermi Prize and the Rumford Medal; membership of exclusive academies like the Royal Society, as well as national scientific associations, such as the American Association for the Advancement of Science; inclusion in directories listing eminent scientists; honorary degrees; invitations to lecture; and finally the citation in published articles of those authors who have previously contributed usefully to the topic under discussion. All these customary forms of scientific behaviour are symbolic expressions of various levels of recognition. Their number and diversity alone testify to the importance of professional recognition in the reward system of science.

The concern on the part of most scientists to elicit a valued response from colleagues in return for research findings, the multiplicity of the forms of professional recognition in science, and the lack of alternative rewards within the scientific community, all support the claim that scientific information is exchanged for recognition. In addition, there are a growing number of studies which show that the more information a scientist supplies, the more recognition is he likely to receive. Thus Cole and Cole (1967) found, for a sample of 120 American physicists, that there was a strong overall relationship between the number of papers published and the amount of recognition received. They also found that, among productive workers, the more recognition their early work attracted, the more often they continued productive in later years. Another interesting study is that in which Zuckerman (1968) compared the publications of a sample of Nobel Prize winners with those of a matched sample of less eminent men. Zuckerman was particularly concerned with the patterns of name ordering among co-authors of joint papers. Working on the assumption that in cases of collaboration most credit will accrue to the author whose name comes first, she compared the two groups. She found that Nobel Prize winners tended to be first authors more often than the controls during their early career when they were striving to establish a reputation, but significantly less often than the controls once their reputation was made and, it is reasonable to infer, further recognition had diminished in value.

These studies, then, show that recognition is broadly distributed within the research community in accordance with the quantity of the information supplied;[1] that receipt of recognition acts as an incentive and leads to higher rates of research productivity; and that the value of further recognition tends to diminish for those who have become eminent. I wish now to suggest in addition that this process of social exchange operates, at least in

[1] The Coles (1967) also studied quality of information, but their argument is rather circular (see Bibliography).

certain circumstances, to maintain intellectual conformity. The main reason for this is that recognition is allocated in accordance with the *perceived* quality of research findings; and clearly the perception of scientific quality will depend on the cognitive and technical preconceptions of those making the judgement. For example, when Cagniard de la Tour, Schwann and, eventually, Pasteur proposed a vitalist interpretation of fermentation, those committed to a purely chemical approach not only refused to recognise that the work had any value, but actually attacked the reputation of the researchers involved by representing them as scientifically incompetent. Many similar although less extreme instances are reported by Hagstrom in his recent survey of the American research community. He sums up his findings on this point in the following words:

> Not only does the desire for recognition induce the scientist to communicate his results; it also influences his selection of problems and methods. He will tend to select problems the solutions of which will result in greater recognition, and he will tend to select methods that will make his work acceptable to his colleagues. (Hagstrom, 1965, pp. 16–17)

Thus recognition is the institutionalised reward for communicating original findings in science. But originality is not valued unconditionally. It is valued and rewarded only in so far as it conforms to current research norms.

Let me summarise the argument presented in this section. People enter science from various social backgrounds and with a variety of motives. Despite social variation among its members, the scientific community is able to maintain certain uniformities of thought and behaviour. This it does, in the first place, by rigorously excluding those unwilling or unable to conform intellectually and by insisting on a narrowly focused education calculated to produce strong commitment to the established body of knowledge. The mental sets created thereby are exceptionally stable. During graduate study the rigidity of scientific education is usually reduced as the neophyte is brought into contact with research developments whose status as scientific knowledge is not conclusively established and as he learns which topics can legitimately be regarded as problematic.

Once his research competence has been explicitly recognised, usually by the award of a Ph.D., the young scientist is formally free to pursue his own intellectual interests – unless he is engaged in large-scale group research. Informally, however, he remains subject to numerous social pressures; in particular, he is faced with the expectation that he will produce research findings acceptable to others working in the same field. Control over the content of his research output is exercised in several ways. In the first instance, close colleagues will warn him if his interests are becoming too deviant, as they warned Pasteur on several occasions. Secondly, funds will be forthcoming only if acceptable research proposals are presented. Finally, the editors and referees of the professional journals act as 'gatekeepers', rejecting submissions which do not conform to current cognitive and technical norms and, as we saw in the actions of Berzelius, Liebig and Wöhler described above, using their position to condemn significantly deviant papers which slip through the screen. In such ways, then, do members of the research community strive to ensure that their colleagues conform to existing cognitive and technical norms. As a result most researchers are led to furnish acceptable information. Such information is rewarded with professional recognition which, in turn, brings other rewards such as promotion, increases in salary, additional research funds, tenure of positions of authority, honorific awards from the wider society, and so on. Thus the exchange of information for recognition is the main institutional mechanism whereby rewards are distributed and intellectual conformity maintained.

It is, of course, true that an exchange of information for recognition occurs in most academic disciplines. The sciences, however, differ from the non-sciences in two important respects. Firstly, the established cognitions of science tend to be expressed in relatively precise mathematical form. Thus Kuhn (1961, p. 55), in an examination of the functions of measurement in science, writes that 'the comparison of numerical predictions . . . has proved particularly successful in bringing scientific controversies to a close. Whatever the price in redefinitions of science, its methods, and its goals, scientists have shown themselves consistently unwilling to compromise the numerical success of their theories.' This stress on cognitive precision in science makes intellectual deviance comparatively obvious and consequently more easily controlled. Secondly, partly as a result of precision, the sciences tend to achieve a high level of professional unanimity which also promotes effective control over intellectual nonconformity. It follows that, *as long as the processes of exchange continue to operate as described so far*, intellectual control in the natural sciences is likely to be peculiarly efficient and to produce a rapid accumulation of information in accord with current cognitive and technical norms. However, as I shall try to show in the next section, social exchange in science also has its own dynamic which regularly generates significant innovation.

4. INNOVATION AND SOCIAL EXCHANGE

In recent years the most widely discussed interpretation of scientific development has been that formulated by T. S. Kuhn in *The Structure of Scientific Revolutions*. In this book Kuhn puts forward a thesis which is entirely consistent with the argument and data presented above. Indeed, several of his notions have already been introduced into the discussion. I shall therefore begin this section with an account of Kuhn's central ideas. Because Kuhn's work has been the subject of much written comment I shall give here only the barest outline.

Kuhn maintains that most scientists most of the time are engaged in 'normal science'. Normal science is research which is guided by paradigms, that is, by a series of related assumptions – theoretical, methodological and empirical – which are generally accepted by those working in a particular area. Although paradigms are to be found in all communities devoted to the pursuit of knowledge, those of the mature sciences are distinctive in that they pose solvable problems about the natural world. This feature is at least partly due to the fact that the paradigms of the advanced sciences are relatively precise and many of their central propositions quantified. Normal research, then, consists in attempting to solve the problems raised by the paradigm without bringing into question its basic assumptions. Because those committed to a scientific paradigm can take their basic cognitive and methodological framework as firmly established, they are able to concentrate on the detailed resolution of that limited range of issues generally regarded as problematic within their research community. As a consequence, normal science leads to the systematic accumulation of relatively precise knowledge.

Kuhn's analysis, as stated so far, furnishes a straightforward answer to the question: how does scientific innovation occur? The answer is that most innovations are relatively minor additions to or modifications of current paradigms and that they are produced by the application of prescribed methods to problems defined as legitimate within the limits of one such paradigm. But this answer is clearly incomplete. It needs to be supplemented with an account of how paradigms are formed and how the transition from one paradigm to another is achieved. This Kuhn does by means of an explicit analogue between scientific development and political revolution. The only way, he argues, in which a radical change of perspective can occur in science is through open rebellion against the existing order of intellectual orthodoxy. Such scientific revolutions are usually provoked by an accumulation of anomalies, which gives rise to pronounced feelings of professional insecurity and a loss of confidence in the current paradigm. An anomaly is a finding which cannot consistently be reconciled with the paradigm-induced expectations governing normal science. All paradigms continually generate anomalies. But normally these failures appear insignificant in the light of past successes and other fruitful work currently in progress. Sooner or later, however, the very efficiency of normal science reveals a growing number of puzzles which simply cannot be answered within the rules of the existing paradigm. The failure of these rules leads to a search for new rules, particularly by the young who are less committed to the old style of thought. Numerous alternative schemes are put forward and the predictability of normal research is undermined, leading to a crisis situation in which there are no generally accepted criteria of scientific excellence. In most cases, out of the competition among the adherents of rival theories, a new paradigm emerges to become generally accepted in the field. Kuhn does not claim to provide a full account of how new paradigms are constructed or how they come to be accepted. Nevertheless, he does maintain that new paradigms are centrally concerned with eliminating those anomalies with which the prior paradigm could not be reconciled; that they change the principles under which legitimate research can be undertaken; and that they are, therefore, bitterly opposed by many of those researchers whose reputation is closely linked to the superseded paradigm.

A new scientific truth does not triumph by convincing its opponents and making them see the light, but rather because its opponents eventually die, and a new generation grows up that is familiar with it.[1]

[1] M. Planck, *Scientific Autobiography* (London : Williams & Norgate, 1950) pp. 33–4.

Kuhn's analysis is broadly consistent with the line of argument proposed in previous sections. In particular, there is a close resemblance between Kuhn's 'paradigms' and what I have called 'cognitive and technical norms'. On the whole, the term 'cognitive and technical norm' seems preferable to that of 'paradigm' for two reasons. Firstly, it leaves empirically open the degree to which the basic assumptions of particular research communities are connected. Unlike the term 'paradigm', which implies that any research tradition involves a series of inseparable preconceptions, it allows for partial and gradual change of intellectual commitment. Secondly, use of the term 'cognitive *norm*' emphasises the similarity between radical innovation and social nonconformity; it draws attention to the part played by social mechanisms in controlling the emergence of new ideas. If intellectual innovation is closely akin to social deviance, it is likely to be associated with systematic variations in the way in which the processes of control operate. Kuhn himself, of course, stresses the importance of scientific education in maintaining intellectual conformity. Normal science, he suggests, is the process of *fitting nature into the boxes provided by a rigid professional education.* Accordingly he argues that radical innovations come predominantly from those who are new to a particular area or new to research altogether and who have not yet acquired a strong commitment to the current paradigm. This argument is, I think, correct as far as it goes, but it ignores entirely the part played by social exchange in maintaining conformity, and consequently fails to consider the possibility that processes of exchange might be involved in the occurrence of innovation. Let me enlarge on this last point.

Research scientists, as we have seen, compete for professional recognition. In fields where a new paradigm has recently been formed, opportunities for recognition are ample. This is so because, as Kuhn indicates, periods of crisis usually end with the selection of a paradigm defining numerous problems with sufficient precision to make them solvable. The ensuing research, which is both competitive and guided by relatively precise intellectual standards, tends either to eliminate rather quickly the more interesting, and therefore more rewarding, problems or to put them aside as anomalous. In the words of Reif (1961, p. 1960): 'Every new discovery . . . results in a burst of intense and very competitive activity. . . . Since so many people concentrate their efforts in one area, the road from the novel to the routine is often travelled in a few months.' Although the length of time involved will vary from one area to another and from one discovery to another, it seems that, after an initial period during which central assumptions are established and basic discoveries made, the topics available within any given area of research produce less and less recognition. As the current paradigm is gradually filled in, those working in the field are likely to look around for more interesting problems. At this point those anomalies, which are *continually* generated by normal science but which are largely ignored whilst interesting and safe topics abound, take on a new significance. As the proportion of problems which are both significant and legitimate diminishes, so anomalies are seen increasingly to be worth investigation and normal research gives way to the less predictable activities of revolutionary science. During periods of revolutionary upheaval, the previous intellectual standards are undermined. It becomes difficult for the researcher to decide which topics are important, which techniques are legitimate, and which results will meet with approval. Thus control by means of social exchange is no longer effective and a great variety of 'wild' ideas are considered. Eventually, however, one of the new perspectives is widely adopted, opening up new areas of profitable study. Cognitive and technical norms are quickly institutionalised through the journals and normal science returns once more.

Consideration of the processes of social exchange in science enables us to improve on Kuhn's analysis, by showing how the very effectiveness of normal science weakens the mechanisms of intellectual control. But the model of scientific development presented so far has one crucial limitation, namely, it is concerned solely with innovation in the sense of radical redefinition of a given field by the members of a fairly stable research community. Such processes of redefinition, although they occur in science as Kuhn has shown, are far from being the predominant pattern of innovation. Thus many instances of scientific innovation are marked not by arduous intellectual redefinition but by intellectual migration followed by the modified application of existing techniques and theories within a different area (Schon, 1963). Similarly, many innovations take the form of a discovery of a new area of ignorance which has not previously been defined at all (Holton, 1962) and within which, consequently, there is no clearly established orthodoxy and little resistance to the emergence

34

of new ideas. Kuhn has failed to include these types of development within his scheme. He has assumed, in contrast, that the membership of any paradigm-group remains fairly stable, apart from the gradual replacement of older researchers by the young. If we accept that there are strong pressures towards intellectual conformity in science, that levels of attainable recognition within any particular area tend to decline, and that research personnel is relatively stable, then we are forced to infer, with Kuhn, that there will be recurrent attempts by the existing members of the paradigm-group to redefine the area of study. However, the assumption that the membership of paradigm-groups usually remains stable is unfounded. In order to make this clear, we must examine a little more closely the networks of social relationships within the basic research community.

Although scientists work in universities and institutes, their primary research audience is composed of all researchers wherever they are located who are working on similar problems and are therefore competent to judge their results and to award recognition (Polanyi, 1962). Thus the social structure of the basic research community is made up of a complex web of *problem networks*. The membership of most networks is widespread geographically but it can be identified in several ways. In the first place, the members of a given network are concerned with a limited range of research problems, for example the difficulties of observing and interpreting pulsars (Meadows and O'Connor, 1971). Secondly, members share certain cognitive and technical norms. Thirdly, and most significantly for purposes of identification, members communicate with each other more frequently than with those outside the network, either through the journals or by less formal means (Price, 1963). Finally, in certain networks, one person or a small number of persons constitutes a central nucleus which exerts considerable influence on the intellectual development of other members (Ben-David and Collins, 1966). Now these problem networks, varying in size from perhaps ten to a hundred members, are important for the present discussion because they are, as Kuhn (1970, p. 178) has recently come to recognise, 'the producers and validators of scientific knowledge'. Research networks are the social units responsible for scientific innovation in the sense that their members encourage or discourage certain lines of work, in the sense that the initial response to research findings is made by a particular network, and in the sense that approved results are taken up and disseminated by the network's members. Furthermore, as Kuhn (1970, p. 176) has also come to accept,

> Scientific communities (i.e. networks) can and should be isolated without prior recourse to paradigms; the latter can then be discovered by scrutinizing the behavior of a given community's members.

However, when we examine these research networks we find that they are, in two ways, *socially unstable*. In the first place, many if not most networks are short-lived. They come into being as unexpected findings generated within one network reveal a new and previously unsuspected area of ignorance. Members of the initial network and others conveniently situated move into the new field in search of interesting and solvable problems. Often within a few years, and sometimes within a few months, the new network breaks up as the initially promising problems are solved or as further provocative areas of ignorance are uncovered. Sooner or later there is a wholesale intellectual migration into newly forming or established networks and the previously thriving field becomes defunct. In certain fields this process has become so pervasive that some researchers have responded by adopting a strategy known as 'skimming the milk', that is, of moving quickly into new areas, making several important contributions before competition becomes too severe, and then moving on as competition increases and the significance of the problems remaining unresolved declines (Hagstrom, 1965). Secondly, even within those areas of research which persist for relatively long periods, there is a constant movement of personnel. This movement into and out of established networks produces a continuous cross-fertilisation of ideas which is often responsible for intellectual change without the kind of redefinition of the field by a stable group envisaged by Kuhn. These processes of growth through escalation and cross-fertilisation are at least as important in accounting for the development of science as is growth through revolution. They are well exemplified in the case of Pasteur who moved continually from one area of research to another, seeking significant problems and attempting to resolve them by the introduction of ideas and techniques developed during his earlier work. There are also certain case studies which I wish to describe because they illustrate this kind of scientific innovation.

36

Let me begin with an example taken from mathematics which is described in two recent papers by Fisher (1966, 1967). Invariant Theory arose in Europe during the 1840s. Within twenty years it became an important and rapidly growing branch of mathematics as the work of Gordan in particular began to open up a whole range of new problems and to attract the attention of increasing numbers of mathematicians. By the 1880s Invariant Theory was generally regarded as an indispensable part of the discipline. However, late in that decade Hilbert, using ideas from a different part of algebra, put forward what he regarded as solutions to the central mathematical problems of the specialty. Despite resistance from those eminent in the field, who were strongly committed to the ideas developed by Gordan and others of the previous generation, Hilbert felt able to claim by 1893 that 'the most important general goals of Invariant Theory are attained'. This claim has been borne out by subsequent events, for although a few isolated individuals continued to work in the area until the 1930s, their occasional publications provoked less and less interest among their existing colleagues or among those entering mathematical research. Furthermore, most of those working in the area during the 1890s quickly withdrew, particularly in Germany where research was most fully institutionalised and competition most extreme. Whereas the rise of Invariant Theory was characterised by an influx of researchers concerned to solve a variety of problems widely regarded as significant, its demise was accompanied by an intellectual migration as those involved sought more promising topics within other research networks. What is striking about the rise and decline of Invariant Theory is not the resistance to innovation within a relatively stable specialty, followed by redefinition of the area in the face of accumulating anomaly, but the relatively slight resistance, followed by rapid movement into alternative fields. Yet perhaps mathematics differs significantly from those disciplines more directly concerned with empirical data. It may be that mathematicians, unlike physical scientists, are not tied to particular sets of problems. It may be that their skills are broad enough to enable them to follow their intellectual interests with unusual ease and that intellectual mobility, so important in explaining the history of Invariant Theory, is a feature peculiar to mathematics. It may be that the elimination of major problems is typically followed in other fields by intellectual redefinition rather than intellectual migration. Let us therefore examine some further examples.

The growth of the phage[1] network within molecular biology, described in a report by Mullins (1968) and a collection of retrospective papers by participants (Cairns *et al.*, 1966), shows not only that there can be high rates of intellectual mobility in disciplines other than mathematics, but also that the arrival of migrants can stimulate far-reaching intellectual development. The origin of the phage network can be traced to a series of discussions during the 1930s among a small group of physicists, including Delbruck, Szilard and others. These men concluded that research in physics was unlikely to reveal any interesting problems for some time to come; that biology seemed to offer the most promising opportunities for using the physical methods with which they were familiar; and that the application of these methods to living matter might generate not only significant biological findings, but also new laws of physics. Considerations such as these led Delbruck and others to undertake research into bacteriophages and problems of biological reproduction. In applying ideas and techniques developed within physics to biological problems, they gradually came to form the nucleus of a research network with a distinct intellectual approach. Evidence of this is found in the collection of articles written by members of the network. There are, for example, references to the 'central dogma' of the phage group, to certain ideas 'considered basic to a new field, later to be called molecular biology', and to the difficulties experienced by phage workers in communicating their ideas to other microbiologists. In addition, Mullins shows that members of the phage network 'tended strongly to read and use ideas only from other phage workers'. To some extent the cognitive and technical structure of the emerging specialty was brought in from other disciplines by the intellectual migrants. But many of the rules which came to govern the study of phages grew out of the attempt to impose order on an area of ignorance in which basic assumptions had yet to be defined. For instance :

> In the summer of 1944 the phage workers under the influence of Delbruck made an important decision. Previously, almost every investigator who worked with bacteriophages had his own private collection of phages and host bacteria. It was therefore almost futile to compare results of different workers,

[1] 'Phage' or 'bacteriophage' means 'bacterial virus'.

or even to gather a satisfying amount of information about one system. Delbruck insisted that we concentrate our attention on the activity of a set of seven phages on the same host. . . . He wanted everyone to work under these standard conditions. . . . (Cairns *et al.*, 1966, p. 73)

Although the specialised approach of the phage network was not always understood by outsiders, there was no strong resistance to its innovations. This, I suggest, was largely because there was no firmly established specialty committed to a prior orthodoxy. Moreover, negative reactions from outside the network had little impact on its development. Thus steady recruitment was ensured when, in 1945, Delbruck initiated a regular summer school to train new entrants attracted by the group's increasingly obvious success. Workers in related areas began to recognise the importance of the group's achievements, which often had implications for their own research. With the discovery of the Watson–Crick structure of DNA there was a sudden increase in government funds, followed by a decade of explosive growth and the eventual award of five Nobel Prizes to members of the group. As we have seen, this series of innovations was set in motion by the transfer of researchers out of physics in search of significant yet solvable problems. But this was merely the first of a continuous series of intellectual migrations. In fact, Mullins describes the movement into and out of the network as 'a rolling, boiling confusion of entries and exits'. He reports that the mean career length in the phage network which he studied was only 3·21 years; and that even those who first entered the field to form its basic intellectual framework stayed in phage on average for less than ten years. He also shows that entrants to phage came from a wide variety of disciplines : physics, chemistry, biophysics and physical chemistry supplied 41·5 per cent of total entrants; bacteriology, medicine, virology, biology and biochemistry produced 44 per cent; while those trained as molecular biologists constituted 14·5 per cent. Although there is a clear web of connections among those engaged in research into phages, the network never became a stable and solidary group. Newcomers entered continuously from a wide range of specialties, worked in the area for a few years and then moved on. This is true even of Delbruck, who actually began to look for new horizons as soon as he saw an effective research framework beginning to take shape.

The examples of Invariant Theory and the phage group establish several points : firstly, that intellectual migration occurs in most if not all scientific disciplines; secondly, that movement tends to occur from areas of declining interest into those with greater opportunities for recognition; and thirdly, that migration can promote radical innovation without engendering serious opposition. Furthermore, Mullins's estimates of movement through the phage network suggest that intellectual mobility may well be a pervasive feature of careers in science. However, Mullins's data are too limited to provide support for any general conclusion on this issue, even when combined with the limited information on scientific mobility available elsewhere (Hagstrom, 1965, p. 173). Accordingly, the best we can do is to examine other available studies of scientific innovation. A study by Zloczower (1966) of developments in German medical science during the last century is useful, not only in providing further documentation of scientific growth through mobility, but also in showing how the internal dynamics of research specialties are influenced by the wider institutional context.

Before 1850 medical science within the German universities was relatively undifferentiated. Within each university there was normally one full professor who, no matter what his area of special competence might be, was responsible for the entire discipline. In the period 1850 to 1900, however, the unified discipline split up into a number of distinct specialties, for example physiology, gynaecology, ophthalmology, and so on. The pattern of development was similar for each of these specialties. Thus Zloczower is able to use physiology to exemplify the general social processes involved. During the first half of the century German medical scientists strove to establish a tradition of cumulative research which would provide a scientific foundation for the practice of medicine. Anatomy was regarded initially as the central discipline, but as physiological knowledge began to accumulate, competence in physiology gradually became a necessary qualification for occupying chairs in anatomy. By the 1840s some of the older anatomists felt unable to take responsibility for physiology. Consequently several separate chairs were founded and occupied by fairly young men competent in the emerging field. The establishment of special chairs opened up new career opportunities for those specialising in physiology. At the same time the rapid growth of interesting findings made it a promising area in which to establish the kind of research reputation necessary for the offer of a chair. As a result, young men were led to specialise in physiological research and thereby to disqualify the non-specialists and to make unavoidable the establishment of separate chairs. Even though many universities would probably have preferred to maintain the existing disciplinary structure, the rivalry between universities to acquire eminent and promising men enabled the latter to insist as a condition of their appointment that they be given a chair in physiology :

> The second half of the nineteenth century thus opened with a struggle for recognition of specific disciplines. The struggle was spearheaded by young men, who as private lecturers had opened up new territory and were loath to dissipate their energies in other than their chosen fields. Characteristically these men were striving not merely for personal recognition; it was not that they were not offered professorships *per se*; what they wanted was the creation of new chairs for their respective disciplines. (1966, p. 42)

Between 1850 and 1870 physiology emerged as a distinct field with a specialised body of knowledge and techniques. The number of separate chairs expanded quickly and the number of discoveries increased dramatically. But there was no accompanying expansion of the German university system. Consequently, by the 1870s virtually all the potential chairs in physiology had been established and occupied by relatively young men. Whereas between 1855 and 1874 twenty-six scientists were appointed to chairs of physiology at German universities, only nine men received such appointments during the next twenty years. Opportunities for research in physiology and for careers less prestigious than those culminating in the award of a university chair continued to expand in the 1870s with the formation of various research institutes. But from the early 1870s there was a marked decline in the opportunity for gaining the main institutionalised symbol of recognition furnished by the German academic system, namely, the university chair. Almost immediately there was a shift of interest within the medical sciences away from physiology. New entrants to medical science chose increasingly to specialise in areas, such as pathology and pharmacology, where the opportuni-

41

ties for gaining recognition for achievement were expanding and where the rate at which discoveries were being made was accelerating. At the same time many private lecturers, whose chances of attaining recognised eminence in physiology were now small, moved into other areas of research. As a result of these processes the rate of innovation in German physiology fell sharply and remained low for a generation.

The development of German physiology during the nineteenth century shows how the university structure can impinge upon the processes of innovation and mobility within the research community. By fostering the rapid expansion of physiology between 1850 and 1870 and the swift recognition of significant achievement, the German university system engendered two decades of intense intellectual productivity in this sphere. The very speed of the expansion, however, eliminated a central source of institutional recognition for most of the next generation of physiologists. The short-term consequences of this were the movement out of physiology by many of those whose careers had been blocked, the diversion of graduates into more promising fields, and the marked decline in the production of significant new results. But the consequences did not end there. For the movement out of physiology had important effects on intellectual innovation elsewhere. For instance, Ben-David and Collins (1966) maintain that it contributed to the emergence of experimental psychology. These authors concentrate in particular on the career of Wundt, who entered physiology in 1857, that is, at the beginning of the period of severe competition for professorial posts. For seventeen years Wundt remained in physiology without receiving the recognition he believed to be his due. At last, in 1875, he accepted the chair of philosophy at Leipzig. Before entering philosophy Wundt had only occasionally criticised the speculative approach dominant in that field at the time. After making this professional transition, however, he attempted to introduce as far as possible the methods of physiology into his new field:

> To preserve his scientific status, he was forced not only to carry out a revolution in philosophy by replacing logical speculation with empirical research, but also to widely advertise the fact that he was in a different kind of enterprise than the traditional philosophers. (1966, p. 463)

This new intellectual enterprise attracted the attention of a number of German philosophers, particularly Brentano, Stumpf, Müller and Ebbinghaus. Thus a new research network grew out of this attempt to apply scientific methods to some of the traditional problems of philosophy. Students from various disciplines and nations quickly attached themselves to the new network. The original problems were speedily redefined, the initial research techniques refined and the growth of modern psychology was set in motion.

The emergence of physiology and experimental psychology in nineteenth-century Germany cannot be understood without reference to the character of the university structure within which these developments took place. Nevertheless, it is possible in these cases as in those discussed previously to ignore, without undue simplification, events occurring outside the academic community. But this kind of simplification is sometimes inappropriate. Let me briefly describe the origins of radio astronomy[1] in order to show how external factors can combine with social processes inside the research community to generate important scientific innovations.

The intellectual origins of radio astronomy can be traced directly to certain developments in physics during the late nineteenth century. In 1873 Clerk Maxwell predicted the existence of electromagnetic radiation either side of the optical spectrum. Four years later Hertz first observed the radio waves predicted by Maxwell. As a result of Hertz's discovery it became conceivable that extra-terrestrial objects emitted radio waves as well as light, that these transmissions could be observed, and therefore that a form of radio astronomy was possible. But the first moves in this direction were not made by astronomers. In 1890 the inventor Edison became the first to try to receive electromagnetic emissions from the sun. A similar attempt was made by the physicist Sir Oliver Lodge in 1894. Neither attempt was successful. After these initial failures interest seems to have declined until, in 1932, Jansky stumbled upon a major discovery. While working for Bell laboratories on the noise level in directional short-wave radio receivers, Jansky observed that there was a constant radio emission which appeared to come from the Milky Way. He con-

[1] This account is based on F. Graham Smith, *Radio Astronomy* (Harmondsworth : Penguin Books, 1960), and on research being carried out by the author in collaboration with Dr D. Edge of the Science Studies Unit, Edinburgh. It deals solely with the U.K.

43

cluded that he was receiving signals from the dense cluster of stars in the centre of our galaxy. His findings were quickly published in an engineering journal and widely publicised by the American mass media. But the research community did not respond. The only man to take up Jansky's work in the 1930s was an amateur astronomer, Karl Reber, who built in his backyard a steerable parabolic reflector with which he established immediately that the radio sky and the optical sky were startlingly different. In retrospect it can be seen that by 1940 Reber's research had created a new branch of astronomy. But the social network which eventually exploited the opportunities revealed by Jansky and Reber was at that moment only just being formed elsewhere in response to political rather than scientific pressures.

At the beginning of the 1939–45 war many of the best physicists in British universities were recruited by government into the Telecommunications Research Establishment. It was quickly decided there that research into radar was likely to prove most productive in military terms. Thus during the war a great deal of attention was paid to the problems associated with transmission of radio waves. Many of the by-products of this research were important for the future of radio astronomy. For example J. S. Hey, following up the work of Jansky and Reber, constructed a radio map of the Northern sky. At the end of the war the physicists left T.R.E., but many of them carried on with the problems of radio transmission. They did not, however, immediately form a new specialty concerned with radio astronomy. On the whole they regarded themselves still as physicists and their subject as 'radio physics'. They took up such problems as the reflection of radio waves from meteor trails and the physical character of the upper atmosphere. Only slowly did they become aware of the immense possibilities involved in detailed study of the radio universe. Gradually, purely physical problems were dropped in favour of astronomical problems. As findings rapidly accumulated, new entrants were attracted to the field; and as the number of researchers grew, so there began to develop the continuous formation and re-formation of problem networks which is so characteristic of scientific specialties.

During the 1950s radio physics became increasingly dependent on astronomy, for example for the measurement of stellar distance which is only possible optically. At the same time the physicists began to respond by supplying useful information to the astronomers, for example information about very distant objects which are optically faint but which emit powerful radio waves. This convergence of research interests became so close that in 1959 the new area of study was officially named 'Radio Astronomy' by the International Telecommunications Union. None the less, the two fields remain institutionally separate. Optical and radio astronomers have different skills. They use distinct techniques and communicate to distinct audiences. In many cases they find it far from easy to understand the details of each other's research. Furthermore, in the United Kingdom at least, most radio astronomers are trained and recruited from departments of physics. This latter fact is a lasting reminder of the way in which radio astronomy arose by accident from the escalation of physics into a new area of ignorance.

The account given above of some of the social processes of scientific innovation stems directly from the prior analysis of social control in science. I shall give a brief summary of the main argument. Scientific research is carried out within small, overlapping social networks. These networks are the units within which intellectual control is exercised and new ideas engendered. Often the members of particular networks share a series of precise cognitive and technical norms which guide research and which facilitate the systematic cumulation of knowledge. But research undertaken within a precise and firmly established cognitive framework cannot continue indefinitely. For as research proceeds, the problems raised become less and less significant and the professional recognition awarded those who provide correct solutions becomes less and less adequate. The decline in the level of available recognition has two important consequences. The first is that researchers become less committed to the existing framework. They become more likely to try to redefine problems and techniques, and more likely to introduce a new and more productive approach to research. Secondly, researchers become more likely to move into other networks which have a greater proportion of significant problems. Such intellectual migration seems, in fact, to occur very frequently. The main reason for this is that research initiated in pursuit of one set of problems regularly produces quite unexpected findings and reveals a whole range of issues previously ignored or unperceived. The emergence of radio astronomy out of industrial and military research or the investigation of genetic codes stemming from the work on DNA are good examples of this process. Where the new problems have not previously been defined there is, of course, no current orthodoxy to be overthrown. Although resistance or strong criticism sometimes occurs on the margins of the emergent network, on the whole its members are free to develop the cognitive/technical structure that seems to them most appropriate and to maintain conformity to their own intellectual norms once these are established. Conformity is maintained by the usual processes of exchange, by the exercise of authority in cases where the network has an eminent founder, through the activities of referees, through the teaching of graduate students, and occasionally by the formation of special training schools. It is important to note, however, that in many cases the emergence of a new network does not depend on the construction of a paradigm or exemplar providing a research model for all subsequent work in the field. Networks derive first from an awareness that there are certain problems, for example concerning the receipt of radio waves from space or the reproduction of phages, which look promising but which are as yet ill-defined. This awareness is followed by the attempt to discover appropriate techniques and to build up piece by piece a suitable theoretical framework. In many instances, therefore, an adequate research framework is achieved only after concerted effort by the members of a previously established network.

The growth of science through the migration of researchers into new areas of ignorance has been exemplified here, in varying forms, by the development of radio astronomy, molecular biology and physiology. Other examples are available in the literature. A closely related social pattern occurs when scientists move into an established network and attempt to apply to its problems preconceptions and techniques acquired elsewhere. In such cases the introduction of new ideas often meets with strenuous resistance. When the cognitive structure of the receiving community is relatively imprecise, it is possible for the newcomers to stress their intellectual uniqueness and to reduce conflict by forming a distinct network. This is exemplified in the emergence of experimental psychology as a result of the influx into philosophy of physiologists and others. When such a social separation does not occur, as when Pasteur moved into one new field after another, trying to impose radical innovations on existing participants, intellectual change tends to take a revolutionary form. But such revolutionary redefinitions of existing fields, unlike those described by Kuhn, are generated by the intrusion of outside ideas rather than by the dynamic effects of paradigm-induced research. It seems indeed, in the light of the present analysis, that revolutions of the kind emphasised by Kuhn will occur only under special conditions. They will occur, firstly, in networks where new and significant problems are no longer being encountered and opportunities for gaining recognition are diminishing. But this condition alone is not sufficient, for one widespread response to diminishing recognition is intellectual migration. Thus, secondly, revolutions are likely to occur where the skills acquired by researchers are not easily transferred. Specificity of skills will inhibit mobility and thereby increase the pressure for radical reinterpretation of the existing area. Thirdly, revolution will tend to occur in networks where cognitions are exceptionally precise and where, consequently, the possibility of gradual intellectual redefinition is limited. These conditions are more likely to occur in the more highly quantified specialties of physics than in fields such as the life sciences.

In the preceding discussion I have emphasised that to understand the growth of scientific ideas we must consider not only the social processes within research networks, but also the relationships between networks. I have, however, greatly simplified the real situation by largely ignoring the ways in which the wider society impinges on the research community. In depicting the emergence of radio astronomy I did describe how the initial breakthrough was an accidental product of industrial research and how government-sponsored work on radar gave birth to the social network which eventually established the field. In addition, the analysis of physiology gave considerable prominence to the impact of the German university system. But such external influences on research have not been treated systematically in this essay. It is clear that any comprehensive model of scientific development would have to specify how economic, political and educational factors link up with those internal dynamics of the research community described above in some detail. I do not, however, intend to consider these problems further. I shall instead turn in the next section to consider how innovation is likely to be distributed within the research community.

5. THE SOCIAL LOCATION OF INNOVATION

In previous sections I have tried to show how processes of social exchange are involved in generating new scientific knowledge as well as in maintaining intellectual conformity. Central to the argument has been the assumption that research is normally guided by cognitive norms and, therefore, that significant innovation often entails intellectual nonconformity. If this is accepted, it should be possible to gain further insight into scientific innovation by trying to judge which kinds of researchers are most likely to be intellectually deviant. In this section I shall try to make such a judgement by applying to scientific innovation certain statements about nonconformity drawn from the literature on social exchange.

The analysis of nonconformity in terms of exchange begins with the claim that most human collectivities can be divided into three status levels.[1] In science this will be three levels of professional recognition. Although this division is analytic in the sense that further subdivisions could be made and to the extent that not all individuals can be unambiguously allocated to a particular level, it is not arbitrary. For this or some similar division is inherent in the exchange strategies generated by the distribution of status or recognition. Each level in the hierarchy presents its occupants with different *costs* and *profits* in situations where it is necessary to choose between conformity and deviance. Consequently, we would expect the frequency of conformity to vary from one level to another. In fact consistent differences in the incidence of nonconformity have been found in various studies and can be summarised in the three propositions below :

1. Members of the middle-status category are least likely to deviate from group opinion or group norms.

[1] G. C. Homans, *Social Behavior: Its Elementary Forms* (New York : Harcourt, Brace & World, 1961).

2. Persons of high and low status are much more likely to be nonconformist.
3. Persons of high status are less likely to deviate from more important norms than from less central norms.

These propositions cannot be regarded as firmly established generalisations. However, they are suggestive for the study of innovation in science. Let us assume that these findings apply to science and try to make sense of them by considering the potential costs and profits attached to the three levels of professional recognition. Those with high scientific reputation will have little to gain by mere conformity. If we assume that the more recognition a person has, the less valuable is any additional unit – and indirect evidence of this has been mentioned above (Zuckerman, 1968) – those at the top are getting decreasing returns from conformity to existing norms or group opinion. This diminution of rewards is likely to be accelerated in science by the tendency for the significance of available problems to decline. At the same time, those with high status have ample resources of recognition to cover the risk involved in nonconformity (Merton, 1968). As we saw in the case of Pasteur, the reputation of an eminent researcher is unlikely to be seriously damaged by the occasional pursuit of a hypothesis regarded as mistaken or even fantastic by his colleagues. There are some grounds, therefore, for expecting such scientists to follow up anomalous observations, to adopt new techniques and interpretative frameworks, and to submit their unexpected findings to the community. They gain little from producing highly predictable results; and by innovating they increase the likelihood of a more acceptable reward without risking any significant alteration to their social position.

There is, however, one important additional consideration. In enduring groups, high levels of recognition usually depend on conformity to certain central norms. If this is true in science, then *radical* innovation, that is, repudiation of basic cognitive norms, would involve considerable risk even for those in the top rank. Furthermore, in cases where eminent men have established their reputation by contributing to the formation of current cognitive standards, radical innovation will put in jeopardy their previous contributions and thereby threaten the very standards on which their eminence depends. It is also true that the mature scientist will have been rewarded for a long period of time for conformity to the existing set of cognitive and technical norms

49

(this of course applies only in relatively stable specialties). We would expect such scientists to develop strong mental sets and a reduced ability to perceive anomalies. It seems reasonable to conclude, therefore, that although persons of high scientific reputation will tend to innovate extensively within the confines of their particular research tradition, they are less likely to introduce radical changes of perspective.

Persons of established middle status in science are likely to be most conservative. They have fewer reserves of recognition on which to draw than persons of high status, and consequently any research failure will do greater damage to their reputation. Furthermore, most of those in this category will have invested considerable time and effort in developing specialised skills. The risks for them of nonconformity are therefore relatively high because it involves the possibility of movement down towards the lowest-status category and the possible redundancy of valuable skills. At the same time, researchers of moderate status have less to gain from successful nonconformity than those at the bottom of the hierarchy. Thus not only are the risks of deviance relatively high but the potential benefits are comparatively low. 'Under these circumstances, where nonconformity offers gains but also serious risk of loss, a man is apt to bet on conformity instead: it cannot hurt his position, it may even help it a little, and it is in either case less risky than the alternative.'[1]

In contrast to the mature scientist of middle rank, the young researcher has everything to gain from nonconformity. He has no reputation to lose. If he does make a serious error, many of his colleagues may respond with sympathetic understanding rather than rejection. And if he comes up with a successful new idea at the outset of his career he will have made a strong bid for eminence on the basis of a minimal investment. In other words, his risks are low and his potential profits exceptionally high. Furthermore, it seems probable that young scientists will believe more firmly than their elders in the myth of scientific impartiality. If this is so, they will be less likely to conceive that revolutionary contributions might be rejected. In addition, although scientific education seems particularly likely to produce rigid mental sets, we would expect the young scientist's perceptual and imaginative capacities to be less firmly fixed than those of men who have been investigating for some years certain narrowly

[1] Homans, *Social Behavior*, p. 353.

defined problems. Moreover, new entrants to research are likely to notice the often considerable divergence between textbook knowledge and current research practice and, as a result, are more likely to reconsider both. Finally, young men entering a 'long-established' field may find that the research problems currently defined as legitimate are too trivial to promise much professional profit. They may, accordingly, come to regard a radical redefinition of the field as a prerequisite for their attaining high-status reputations. I suggest, therefore, that young scientists or, more broadly, new entrants to specialties, are especially likely to perceive anomalies, pursue them and submit their findings to the research community.

This generalisation has been derived by applying some of the notions of exchange analysis to the study of nonconformity to cognitive and technical norms. It coincides, however, very closely with Kuhn's (1962, pp. 89–90) assertion that 'Almost always the men who achieve . . . fundamental inventions of a new paradigm have been either very young or very new to the field whose paradigm they change . . . obviously these are the men who, being little committed by prior practice to the traditional rules of normal science, are particularly likely to see that those rules no longer define a playable game and to conceive another set that can replace them.' Typically, Kuhn stresses that innovators are likely to be those whose perceptual framework is less rigid because they have not been fully socialised into the relevant specialty. Although I would not deny that innovation is connected with the extent to which different categories of scientists have internalised current standards, I have suggested above that it also depends on the distribution of professional rewards and the way in which divergent exchange strategies are dispersed throughout the scientific community.

There exists considerable but unsystematic evidence in support of the claim that significant innovations come disproportionately from young researchers at the foot of the scientific hierarchy and others on the margins of research networks (Ben-David, 1960b). Indeed, several instances have been described above. Let me just mention the foray of the inventor Edison into radio astronomy; the favourable response of the amateur astronomer Reber to Jansky's discovery; Wundt's redefinition of the problems and methods of speculative philosophy; and Pasteur's advocacy of the vitalist theory of fermentation and the germ theory of contagious

51

diseases. These are all examples of major innovations being initiated or taken up by men on the margins of the research network centrally involved. The generalisation that there is a connection between innovation and social marginality can be given a plausible interpretation in terms of risks and profits, along the lines adopted above in relation to low-status researchers. Indeed, low status within a research network is to be regarded as one form of marginality. As it stands, however, the generalisation is too crude to be open to rigorous test, and the interpretation in terms of exchange is too loose to prevent an indefinite series of modifications in the face of 'contrary' evidence. The analysis offered here, then, is intended to be no more than suggestive.

The discussion so far in this section has been concerned primarily with radical innovation in relatively stable networks. But we know from earlier sections that many innovations do not take this revolutionary form. They occur instead as researchers abandon areas of declining interest and move either into new areas of ignorance or into other networks which have promising problems. Such intellectual migration may well be much easier for eminent scientists than the reconceptualisation of existing issues. In the first place, it does not require that change of *Gestalt* which, as Kuhn stresses, the committed scientist finds so agonising. Indeed, in most cases it seems that the migratory scientist can retain a strong commitment to the intellectual assumptions of his initial field of study as well as a conviction that these assumptions alone can lead to a proper exploitation of the emerging field. This can be seen clearly in the cases of Pasteur, Wundt and Delbruck. Secondly, intellectual migration in itself, unlike participation in a scientific revolution, involves no threat to the eminent researcher's past contribution to knowledge. His reputation is likely to suffer only if the new departure produces meagre results. But in this respect the eminent man has everything in his favour (Merton, 1968; Reif and Strauss, 1965). He will have little difficulty in obtaining research funds. He will have extensive knowledge of developments in other fields and will be able to make an informed judgement as to which areas are most suitable for the application of his particular skills. Furthermore, assuming that he occupies a prominent position in a university department or research institute, he will be able to attract graduate students into the area and direct their attention to problems linked to his own.

He will also have automatic access to the journals, and by sponsoring the work of his protégés will be able to promote quick expansion of the field. Finally, the active participation of one or more eminent men in a new field will also ensure that its findings are given careful consideration by outsiders, even if these findings appear to conflict with bodies of knowledge firmly established in neighbouring areas. In general, then, intellectual mobility seems to be relatively easy for the top-level scientist. The situation facing those without an established reputation is, however, quite different. Funds for speculative projects are less easily obtained. Information on interesting developments in other fields is less available. And resistance from journals, in the absence of an eminent sponsor, is more probable. Thus it seems likely that in instances where researchers move into new fields and form new networks, eminent men of high repute will tend to take the lead. This was clearly so in those major innovations in which Pasteur was involved. It was also true of the research network set in motion by Wundt and the small band of German philosophers. Similarly, Mullins shows unambiguously that as the processes of recruitment into the phage group stabilised, so the mature first entrants were followed by much younger men.

The argument presented in this section can be summarised as follows. Scientists' research strategies vary with their position on the prestige hierarchy of the research community. Whether or not scientists located at a particular level introduce radically new ideas or move into emerging fields depends largely on the costs and profits entailed.[1] It appears that the balance of costs and profits tends to favour the emergence of innovation at the top and bottom of the hierarchy. Intellectual nonconformity is promoted at the top, firstly by the tendency for problems to decline in significance within a given field, and secondly by the tendency for further units of recognition to become less and less valuable to the recipient. The reputations of eminent men, however, are closely associated with the existing body of knowledge to which they have made a significant contribution. There is a tendency, therefore, for them to resist revolutionary reconceptualisation of their own field. Thus it seems likely that scientific revolutions will usually be led by relative newcomers to research or by entrants from other networks. The latter will often be men of established reputation in their field of origin, for whom intellectual mobility

[1] Measured in terms of professional recognition.

has been relatively easy. In fact intellectual migration, whether into established networks or into virgin areas, will normally be led by mature researchers of known repute. These men use their eminence to attract funds and graduate students; and in various ways they try to use their existing knowledge and techniques as a point of departure for the construction of the new intellectual framework. As the significant problems revealed by the network are resolved, so those eminent researchers who helped to found the field as well as those who achieved eminence during its formative period tend to move on into unexplored territory. And so the escalation of science continues.

6. STATEMENT OF THE MAIN ARGUMENT AND ITS LIMITATIONS

The basic research community is divided into a great variety of social groupings. At the most general level it is made up of broad academic disciplines, such as physics, chemistry and mathematics. These disciplines are largely responsible for passing on the body of established knowledge to each new generation of researchers. On the whole this knowledge is transmitted with considerable intellectual rigidity, so that most of those entering a given discipline at one point in time will share a common and largely unquestioned frame of reference. As these new entrants become actively engaged in research, their intellectual concerns become increasingly specialised. Consequently, they find that they are members of a specialty within the parent discipline, for example high-energy physics, solid-state physics, steroid chemistry, and so on. Often these scientific specialties have various formal organs, such as conferences, journals, funding committees and possibly specialised training courses and university departments. By means of these organs the members of any specialty are able to exercise some control over the work of their colleagues and to attempt to maintain acceptable levels of conformity to cognitive and technical norms widespread within the specialty. However, all specialties are further divided into various problem networks. Most scientists are members of several such networks, but they seldom belong to more than a few of those extant in their specialty. Furthermore, the problems of different networks vary sufficiently to limit the scientific competence and interest of most researchers to the few networks directly bordering their own (Polanyi, 1962). As a result, it is within the problem network that intellectual control is largely exercised and new ideas either approved or rejected.

Research networks vary considerably in size and duration. In

55

large and enduring networks cognitive and technical norms tend to become firmly established. When this happens, researchers gain recognition by supplying results which are original yet which do not depart significantly from the generally accepted framework. This is the process which Kuhn calls 'normal science'. But normal science is necessarily self-terminating for two reasons: firstly, because researchers compete with each other for the scarce resource of professional recognition, and secondly, because this competition ensures that as significant problems are eliminated, so the rewards for normal research within any given area decline. In networks which have a highly precise cognitive structure and where opportunities for mobility are low, this diminution of professional returns sometimes leads new entrants and other marginals to rebel against the current intellectual orthodoxy. More usually, however, those who are not receiving adequate professional rewards change the focus of their research interests and join a more promising network where, as far as possible, they attempt to make use of knowledge and techniques acquired during their previous work. In many instances this process of intellectual migration promotes a radical redefinition of an existing area of study, often in the face of strong resistance from those already engaged in the field. Just as often, however, intellectual migrants move into those new areas of ignorance which develop unpredictably on all research fronts. This second type of migration leads to the formation of a new social network and the gradual construction of a set of cognitive and technical standards defining the new area of investigation. In most cases it meets with less extreme resistance. Despite certain differences, however, both kinds of scientific migration tend to be led by men of some eminence, who are followed by younger researchers in pursuit of interesting problems and high levels of professional recognition.

The description I have offered above of scientific innovation has been composed from various studies of developments within different scientific areas at different points in time. In attempting to make sense of these studies I have stressed those factors which are common to a whole range of innovations rather than those which are found only in a few instances. Consequently, although I have included as much concrete material as space allows, the interpretation remains rather general. What it does, I hope, is to draw attention to certain social processes which are involved in a great variety of scientific innovations. In addition to being somewhat general, the discussion above is, in places, speculative. For example, in interpreting the onset of scientific revolutions and the occurrence of intellectual migration, I have inferred that in the course of normal science there is a tendency for available rewards to decline in value. This inference is plausible in the light of the evidence of an exchange of information for recognition in science. It does not, however, have direct and independent empirical support. The argument developed here is also incomplete, in so far as it ignores the impact on basic research of influences originating outside the research community. There can be no doubt that external factors have always been important and that any full account of scientific development would have to consider systematically how such factors affect the distribution of professional recognition and the formation of problem networks. Finally, I have ignored in this essay the whole problem of recruitment into science. Until recently there has been a cumulative expansion of research personnel in Western societies. There are signs, however, that the rapid exponential growth is coming to an end (Price, 1963). If this trend continues, it may well alter significantly the character of professional competition in science and thereby change the social processes at present leading to scientific innovation. Although such considerations have important implications for the analysis presented above, I have simply left them out of the discussion. These, then, are some of the more obvious deficiencies of this brief study in the sociology of science.

BIBLIOGRAPHY

B. Barber, *Science and the Social Order* (London: Allen & Unwin, 1953). An early attempt to make a comprehensive statement about the sociology of science. Still useful in places, but increasingly out of date.

——, 'Sociology of Science: A Trend Report and Bibliography', *Current Sociology*, v 2 (1956) 91–153. A statement of the aims and achievements of the sociology of science.

—— and W. Hirsch (eds), *The Sociology of Science* (New York: The Free Press, 1962). A valuable collection of papers.

J. Ben-David, 'Scientific Productivity and Academic Organization in Nineteenth Century Medicine', *American Sociological Review*, xxv (1960*a*) 828–43. Reprinted in Barber and Hirsch (eds), *The Sociology of Science*. An interesting comparative study in which it is argued that the rate of scientific productivity varies directly with the level of scientific competition.

——, 'Roles and Innovations in Medicine', *American Journal of Sociology*, lxv (May 1960*b*) 557–68 . An attempt is made to show how, in the cases of bacteriology and psychoanalysis, occupants of positions on the margins of the research network were responsible for introducing significant innovations.

——, 'Scientific Growth: A Sociological View', *Minerva*, ii (1964) 455–76. A review of A. C. Crombie (ed.), *Scientific Change* (London: Heinemann, 1963). Particularly interesting for its comments on the work of T. S. Kuhn.

——, *The Scientist's Role in Society*, Foundations of Modern Sociology Series (Englewood Cliffs, N.J.: Prentice-Hall, 1971). A detailed examination of the social conditions determining the level of scientific activity and shaping the roles of scientists and the organisation of science in different countries at different times.

—— and R. Collins, 'Social Factors in the Origins of a New Science: The Case of Psychology', *American Sociological*

Review, xxxi (Aug 1966) 451–65. A useful study of the way in which developments in physiology and philosophy contributed to the emergence of experimental psychology.

J. Cairns, G. Stent and J. Watson, *Phage and the Origins of Molecular Biology* (Cold Spring Harbor, N.Y.: Cold Spring Harbor Laboratory of Quantitative Biology, 1966). A valuable sourcebook used extensively in the paper by Mullins cited below.

T. N. Clark, 'Institutionalisation of Innovations in Higher Education', *Administrative Science Quarterly*, xiii (1968) 1–25. An attempt to state succinctly a conceptual framework for the study of the processes whereby innovations are institutionalised.

S. Cole and J. Cole, 'Scientific Output and Recognition: A Study in the Operation of the Reward System in Science', *American Sociological Review*, xxxii (June 1967) 377–90.

—— and ——, 'Visibility and the Structural Bases of Awareness of Scientific Research', *American Sociological Review*, xxxiii (June 1968) 397–412. Two invaluable studies of scientific communication and exchange. One possible defect in research design, namely, the indices for 'recognition' and for 'information', tend to overlap in the 1967 paper.

J. B. Conant, *Science and Common Sense* (New Haven: Yale U.P., 1951). A clear discussion of the ways in which scientists operate and how their work impinges on society.

S. Cotgrove and S. Box, *Science, Industry and Society* (London: Allen & Unwin, 1970). Includes a study of science undergraduates and an examination of how science students choose their careers.

D. Crane, 'Scientists at Major and Minor Universities', *American Sociological Review*, xxx (Oct 1965) 699–714. A study of the effects of academic affiliation on the receipt of professional rewards in science. Although the sample includes political scientists as well as psychologists and biologists, there is virtually no discussion of differences between disciplines.

——, 'The Gatekeepers of Science: Some Factors Affecting the Selection of Articles for Scientific Journals', *American Sociologist*, ii (1967) 195–201. An interesting attempt to examine how journals influence the processes of scientific communication.

——, 'Social Structure in a Group of Scientists', *American Sociological Review*, xxxiv (June 1969) 335–52. A valuable study of the social ties within one problem network. A significant limitation of this study, however, is its choice of a problem area easily understood by the author, namely, rural sociology.

K. J. Downey, 'The Scientific Community: Organic or Mechanical?', *Sociological Quarterly,* x 4 (fall 1969) 438–54. A discussion of the social structure of the research community in the light of Durkheim's typology. It is concluded that the mechanical model of science is most appropriate.

C. Fisher, 'The Death of a Mathematical Theory', *Archives for History of Exact Sciences,* III (1966) 137–59.

——, 'The Last Invariant Theorists', *Archives of European Sociology,* VIII (1967) 216–44. Two valuable papers on the decline of a mathematical specialty.

J. Gaston, 'Big Science in Britain: A Sociological Study of the High Energy Physics Community', unpublished Ph.D. thesis (Yale University, 1969). A useful study of the British members of one particular specialty.

——, 'The Reward System in British Science', *American Sociological Review,* XXXV 4 (Aug 1970) 718–32. The distribution of professional rewards among high-energy physicists in Britain. Some attention is paid to the differentiation of experimental and theoretical roles.

A. de Grazia *et al., The Velikovsky Affair* (New York: University Books, 1966). An invaluable account of one of the most intriguing and revealing episodes in the recent history of science.

W. O. Hagstrom, 'Traditional and Modern Forms of Scientific Teamwork', *Administrative Science Quarterly,* IX (1964) 241–63. A considered assessment of the extent to which traditional forms of teamwork are being replaced.

——, *The Scientific Community* (New York: Basic Books, 1965). By far the best available account of the social relationships within the research community. Essential reading for those interested in control and innovation in science.

B. W. G. Holt, 'Social Aspects in the Emergence of Chemistry as an Exact Science: The British Chemical Profession', *British Journal of Sociology,* XXI 2 (June 1970) 181–99. A useful comparison of the emergence of chemistry in Germany and in the U.K.

G. Holton, 'Models for Understanding the Growth and Excellence of Scientific Research', in S. R. Graubard and G. Holton (eds), *Excellence and Leadership in a Democracy* (New York: Columbia U.P., 1962). The analysis in this article of growth through escalation is an important contribution to the field.

L. Hudson, *Contrary Imaginations* (London: Methuen, 1966).
——, *Frames of Mind* (London: Methuen, 1968). These two books present a series of studies of the psychological characteristics of schoolboys. They are significant here owing to the finding that science students, when compared with arts students, tend to be more convergent, more reliant on the syllabus, and so on.

F. R. Jevons, *The Teaching of Science* (London: Allen & Unwin, 1969). This is a thorough survey of the literature on scientific education and an attempt to develop some of the practical implications.

N. Kaplan (ed.), *Science and Society* (Chicago: Rand McNally, 1965). A useful collection of essays.

T. S. Kuhn, 'The Essential Tension: Tradition and Innovation in Scientific Research', in C. W. Taylor and F. Barron (eds), *Scientific Creativity* (New York: Wiley, 1963). A discussion of scientific education and creativity in the light of the distinction between normal and revolutionary science. This paper was first published in 1959.

——, 'The Function of Measurement in Modern Physical Science', in H. Woolf (ed.), *Quantification* (New York: Bobbs-Merrill, 1961) pp. 31–61. A discussion of scientific quantification in the light of the distinction between normal and revolutionary science.

——, *The Structure of Scientific Revolutions* (Chicago U.P., 1962). A fundamental contribution. A systematic attempt to view the cognitive structure of science in relation to its social structure. A second edition published in 1970 contains an important additional chapter in which Kuhn moves further away from a history of ideas towards a sociology of science.

I. Lakatos and A. Musgrave (eds), *Criticism and the Growth of Knowledge* (Cambridge U.P., 1970). A collection of comments on Kuhn's work and commentaries on issues raised by Kuhn's work.

H. Martins, 'The Kuhnian "Revolution" and its Implications for Sociology', in A. H. Hanson, T. Nossiter and S. Rokkan (eds), *Imagination and Precision in Political Analysis* (London: Faber, 1971). A wide-ranging and stimulating discussion of Kuhn's work and its implications.

A. J. Meadows and J. G. O'Connor, 'Bibliographical Statistics as a Guide to Growth Points in Science', *Science Studies,* 1 1 (Jan 1971) 95–9. A useful analysis of the emergence of a research network concerned with pulsars.

R. K. Merton, 'Priorities in Scientific Discovery', *American Sociological Review,* xxii (1957) 635–59. Reprinted in *The Sociology of Science*, pp. 447–85. A most important article from which stems a whole tradition of research on the reward system of science exemplified in the work of Hagstrom, Crane and S. and J. Cole.

——, 'Singletons and Multiples in Scientific Discovery', *Proceedings of the American Philosophical Society,* cv 5 (Oct 1961) 470–86. Attention is drawn in this paper to the frequency of independent multiple discoveries in science and the significance of this fact for the sociology of science.

——, 'The Matthew Effect in Science', *Science,* clix (5 Jan 1968) 56–63. It is argued that scientific recognition is distributed in such a way that eminent researchers obtain further recognition more easily than those who have not yet made their mark; and that accumulated recognition facilitates the movement of eminent men into new fields of inquiry.

M. J. Mulkay, 'Some Aspects of Cultural Growth in the Natural Sciences', *Social Research,* xxxvi 1 (spring 1969) 22–52. A critique of some of the dominant themes in the functionalist interpretation of scientific innovation and an attempt to outline an alternative approach.

—— and B. S. Turner, 'Over-production of Personnel and Innovation in Three Social Settings', *Sociology,* v 1 (Jan 1971) 47–61. A comparison of innovations in religion, painting and science.

N. Mullins, 'The Prelude to Scientific Specialties: Cluster Development within Patterns of Association among Scientists', paper given at the 1968 meeting of the American Sociological Association. A most interesting study of the formation of the phage network.

M. Polanyi, 'The Republic of Science', *Minerva,* 1 1 (1962) 54–73. A valuable discussion of the nature of intellectual control in science. Polanyi examines a wide range of related issues in *Personal Knowledge* (London: Routledge & Kegan Paul, 1958).

D. J. de Solla Price, *Big Science, Little Science* (New York: Columbia U.P., 1963). This book assesses the rate at which modern science has grown and describes some of the accompanying changes in the structure of the scientific community. Essential reading.

——, 'Networks of Scientific Papers', *Science,* cxlix (30 July 1965) 510–15. One example of the way in which Price has tried to trace communication networks among scientists.

F Reif, 'The Competitive World of the Pure Scientist', *Science,* cxxxiv (15 Dec 1961) 1957–62. A fascinating description of the formation of new means of communication in response to extreme competition.

—— and A. Strauss, 'The Impact of Rapid Discovery upon the Scientist's Career', *Social Problems,* xii 5 (1965) 297–311. A perceptive account of the consequences of competition and rapid discovery for the individual researcher.

D. Schon, *Displacement of Concepts* (London: Tavistock, 1963). This book provides a useful supplement to that of Kuhn. It begins to formulate a conception of intellectual change in terms of the cross-fertilisation of ideas and the metaphorical extension of existing concepts to new areas.

G. M. Swatez, 'The Social Organisation of a University Laboratory', *Minerva,* viii 1 (Jan 1970) 36–58. This paper describes some of the social relations within a high-energy physics laboratory in which participants try to combine individualism with large-scale organisation.

J. D. Watson, *The Double Helix* (New York: Atheneum Publishers, 1968). A personal account by one of the participants of the events which led to the discovery of the structure of DNA. Watson's early career is described briefly in Cairns *et al., Phage and the Origins of Molecular Biology,* cited above.

R. Whitley, 'Communication Nets in Science: Status and Citation Patterns in Animal Physiology', *Sociological Review,* xvii 2 (July 1969) 219–33. A study of patterns of communication and distribution of rewards within a specific specialty.

J. Ziman, *Public Knowledge: The Social Dimension of Science* (Cambridge U.P., 1968). A wide-ranging discussion of the social relations of science by a scientist still engaged in physical research.

A. Zloczower, *Career Opportunities and the Growth of Scientific Discovery in 19th-Century Germany, with Special Reference to Physiology* (The Eliezer Kaplan School of Economics and Social Sciences, Hebrew University of Jerusalem, 1966). A detailed and valuable study of changes in the academic structure of German medicine during the last century.

H. A. Zuckerman, 'Nobel Laureates in Science: Patterns of Productivity, Collaboration and Authorship', *American Sociological Review*, xxxII (June 1967) 391–403. An investigation of the publication practices of Nobel laureates before and after receipt of the prize.

——, 'Patterns of Name Ordering among Authors of Scientific Papers', *American Journal of Sociology*, LXXIII (1968) 276–91. An examination of the ways in which the ordering of authors' names is used to allocate responsibility and credit among collaborators.